ISBN 978-0-260-52968-8
PIBN 11122092

1 MONTH OF
FREE
READING

at
www.ForgottenBooks.com

By purchasing this book you are eligible for one month membership to ForgottenBooks.com, giving you unlimited access to our entire collection of over 1,000,000 titles via our web site and mobile apps.

To claim your free month visit:
www.forgottenbooks.com/free1122092

English
Français
Deutsche
Italiano
Español
Português

www.forgottenbooks.com

Mythology Photography **Fiction**
Fishing Christianity **Art** Cooking
Essays Buddhism Freemasonry
Medicine **Biology** Music **Ancient**
Egypt Evolution Carpentry Physics
Dance Geology **Mathematics** Fitness
Shakespeare **Folklore** Yoga Marketing
Confidence Immortality Biographies
Poetry **Psychology** Witchcraft
Electronics Chemistry History **Law**
Accounting **Philosophy** Anthropology
Alchemy Drama Quantum Mechanics
Atheism Sexual Health **Ancient History**
Entrepreneurship Languages Sport
Paleontology Needlework Islam
Metaphysics Investment Archaeology
Parenting Statistics Criminology
Motivational

LAND REDISTRIBUTION IN
MEXICO

U.S FOREIGN AGRICULTURAL SERVICE.
U.S. DEPARTMENT OF AGRICULTURE
MARCH 1961   FAS - M 112

LAND REDISTRIBUTION IN MEXICO

Contents

The governments of Latin America are looking closely these days at the patterns of land ownership in their countries and the uses to which land is being put. Land-redistribution programs are now in effect in several of the countries, and are being planned in others.

Mexico was the first of the Latin American countries to put into effect such an agrarian reform program. That program is not yet complete, but is a continuing one. President Adolfo López Mateos has announced the intention of his administration to intensify the agrarian program and the distribution of land until every landless peasant has received a plot of his own.

The reform program is based partly on the ancient systems of land tenure that existed among the native population when the Spaniards arrived, partly on systems introduced by the Spanish conquerors and on other European influences, and, to a great extent, on Mexican ideas and Mexican experience. The present pattern of reform grew out of the Revolution of 1910. It developed gradually as objectives were slowly defined and methods were found for implementing them until it reached its peak in the mid-1930's. During the past several years the program has been modified and is now receiving renewed emphasis.

Land Reform Begins

Unrest throughout the rural areas of Mexico was the fuel that fed the flames of revolution back in 1910. This revolution broke out first as a political uprising aimed at ending the 34-year dictatorship of Porfirio Días with a battle cry of "effective suffrage and no re-election". But this slogan made little appeal to the great mass of the rural population. They were starved for land -- and it was estimated that about 90 percent of them had no land whatsoever. It was only when the promise of land was held out to these farm people that the movement had meaning for them, and they rallied to the call of "land and liberty" and the revolt, which started out as a political movement, soon became an agrarian revolution.

As success came for the Revolutionaries, first steps were taken to make good the promises of land for the landless. On January 6, 1915, the Carranza Government issued a decree that marked the beginning of the agrarian reform program. This decree stated the philosophy of the reform: That villages had the right to receive sufficient land for their needs and that such lands could be expropriated from adjacent properties. The agrarian program was later incorporated into Article 27 of the Constitution

of 1917, which is the legal basis for all subsequent agrarian legislation.
Much of the actual agrarian program itself has been operated under a series
of Agrarian Codes, the first of which was adopted in 1934 toward the end of
the administration of President Abelardo Rodriquez. The Code was modified
several times during the administration of General Cárdenas and a second
Agrarian Code was issued in October 1940, a few weeks before the end of that
administration. A third Code, which is still in force, was issued in
December 1942.

Land Distribution Methods and Basis for Them

The original reform program provided for three types of grants:

1. By restitution, or grants made to restore to a community lands
which formerly belonged to it. These require that the community furnish
proof of its right to the lands in question. Although at the beginning of
the agrarian program, this was looked upon as the most important form of
grant, the difficulties involved soon made its application almost impossible
and it has accounted for a very minor fraction of the total amount of land
distributed up to the present time.

2. By dotación, or those made as an outright grant requiring no evidence of former ownership of the land by the community. This type soon
became the most important vehicle for the distribution of land under the
agrarian program and has been responsible for about 80 percent of the total
area distributed.

3. By amplification, which are grants actually of the same type as
those by dotación, except that they apply when the community has previously
received a grant which is considered insufficient for its needs.

A dotación consists of the expropriation of that portion of a private
property exceeding certain size limits and the granting of the expropriated
land to a village claiming it, provided the village is located within a
radius of 7 kilometers (4 miles) of the property to be expropriated.

In order for a community to qualify for a grant by dotación, a request
must be made by not less than 20 native-born Mexicans residing in the community asking for the grant. The request is presented through the proper
channels, an investigation is made of the qualifications of the claimants
and of the availability of the affectible land (land within a private
holding in excess of certain size limitation), and a provisional decision is
made by the governor of the State in which the land is located. If the
decision is favorable, the claimants are given provisional possession of the
lands and the case is turned over to the Department of Agrarian and
Colonization Affairs. This Department hears evidence from the landowners
and from the claimants, but final decision is made by the President of the
Republic.

The maximum limits for inaffectible private holdings are 100 hectares
of irrigated or humid land (250 acres); 200 hectares of unirrigated land

- 2 -

(500 acres); 150 hectares (370 acres) of cotton; 300 hectares (740 acres) in bananas, sugarcane, coffee, cacao, fruit trees, henequen, and a few other perennial crops; or the amount of land required to maintain 500 head of cattle. This does not mean that all holdings in excess of the above limits are automatically expropriated, but they are subject to expropriation if a request is made by a legally qualified village within the 7-kilometer radius.

When a private property is affected by an agrarian dotación, the owner is allowed to choose the location, within his property, of the land he is permitted to retain. The remainder is expropriated by the government and turned over to the requesting community as an ejido. The land is given free of any charge to the recipients. The majority of the ejidos are of the so-called individual type. This means the land is distributed to the ejidatarios who work their plots individually. These plots cannot be sold or mortgaged, but they remain in the possession of the ejidatario for life, provided he works the land, and may be bequeathed by him to one of his heirs. These conditions are similar to those placed on the possession of land in the altepetlallis of pre-Conquest Mexico.

Before the arrival of the Spaniards, for example, the most prevalent form of land tenure was the land-holding village. To each village was assigned an area of land surrounding it, including cropland, timberland, and hunting grounds. This area was known as altepetlalli, or town land, and was divided among the heads of families, each of whom received a tillable plot. The assignment of these plots was in charge of the head of the clan or the village and was subject to conditions similar to those under which land is granted to the ejidos at the present time:

1. The recipient was required to till the soil regularly. If a plot was not cultivated for 2 years in succession it was subject to forfeiture.

2. No written titles were given but use of the plot could be transmitted from father to son.

3. If a family moved away from the village or became extinct, the plot returned to the clan and was reassigned to others or held in reserve for future needs.

Other Land Distribution Practices

Most of the land distributed in past years was through "restitution", "dotación", and "amplification", of which dotación was the most important. However, in the past 2 years a large proportion was granted through other methods, principally through the establishment of new centers of population. The chief difference between this method and dotación is that in the latter case there is no movement of the population to other areas.

Should there be no land subject to expropriation within the 7-kilometer radius, a grant by "dotación" is not possible. In such a case the group claiming land may be transported to another area where land is available and a new center of population is thus established. This method is based on Article 100 of the Agrarian Code which provides that "the creation of a new center of population shall take place when the needs of a group qualified to constitute such a center may not be satisfied through the procedures of restitution, dotación, or amplification of ejidos. . ."

The increasing use of this method of granting land is a recognition of the fact that land available for distribution is now scarce in the areas of greatest population density. After 45 years of agrarian reform, most private properties in these areas have been reduced by successive expropriations to the limits of an "inaffectible" holding, as defined by Article 104 of the Agrarian Code. Such properties are not subject to expropriation under present legislation.

The rest of the land distributed during the past 2 years also included lands settled under the Federal Law of Colonization and the legislation for the disposal of national lands. Under an old law of August 2, 1923, national lands may be donated to farmers who have been occupying them on good faith for a period of about 5 years. These lands are not settled either as ejidos or as colonies. They are given away and become the private property of the recipients.

The Federal Law of Colonization was published in the Diario Oficial of January 25, 1947, replacing the Colonization Law of 1926. Under this law, agricultural colonies may be established on rural land, national or private, capable of being improved and planted in agricultural crops. Provision is made for expropriating such lands provided that they are not already being used adequately for agricultural production, are not in the forest reserves, and are not exempted from expropriation under Article 27 of the Constitution.

The Department of Agrarian and Colonization Affairs and individuals or legally constituted Mexican associations may carry out a colonization program, independently or on a cooperative basis. Colonization proceedings may be initiated by the government or at the request of a private promoter. After initiation of a project, determination must be made that the needs for ejido grants of the villages in the zones to be colonized have been satisfied. The President may then issue a declaration of public utility after publication of which the lands included in the project shall be considered inaffectible by ejido grants for a period of 5 years. The lands included in such declaration will remain out of the market for any other purpose and, if they are national lands, those who may be occupying them, or who may have applied for them, shall have no other right except to be preferred as settlers and their possession of the land shall be respected up to the maximum area assigned to lots in the colony.

These lands are settled not as ejidos, but as "colonies". The colonists are given 10 years to pay for the land, and once they complete payment are given full ownership of the land. All transfers, mortgages, or encumbrances of any form placed on a lot must be in accordance with the provisions of the Law of Colonization, and persons to whom land is transferred must fulfill the requirements for colonists in a particular colony.

A new policy for land settlement under the Colonization Law has been announced by the Agrarian Department. According to this policy, settlers under the Colonization Law must be selected from among campesinos con derechos a salvo (peasants with reserved rights). These are landless persons who qualified for land under an agrarian expropriation within 4 miles of their village and to whom no land was given because the area expropriated was not sufficient for all those who qualified. In such a case a list is made of these persons and they are considered as having reserved agrarian rights. The number of these people has been estimated at from half a million to 1 million. Most of them are located in the Central Plateau, principally in the States of Michoacán, Guanajuato, and Querétaro. Formerly, colonization projects could be carried out with any individuals who were willing to settle in the area, regardless of whether they were landless or met any of the other requirement of the agrarian law.

In order to facilitate the movement from areas of great population density to the more sparsely populated regions, the Agrarian Department is offering special inducements to those with reserved agrarian rights. Under the new program small groups of about 25 men are transported to the area to be settled, where they are given $.80 per day until such time as they harvest the first crop. Upon arrival at the colony the settlers first help to build a structure out of such materials as may be available in the region. This first construction is intended for subsequent use as a schoolhouse, but serves temporarily as living quarters for the settlers. Once the schoolhouse is finished the rest of the men who are to form the settlement arrive. Some devote themselves to building houses and the others to clearing and planting the land. As the houses are finished the families are brought to the settlement. The land is sold to the settlers considerably below the market price of the land with a long time to pay, beginning a year after the first harvest. Settlers must also repay to the government the amount of $.80 per day advanced to them as well as the cost of transportation for themselves and their families, their share of depreciation of the machinery used, the cost of the fuel, and the wages paid to tractor operators and mechanics. The amount received by the government in payment for the land is to be used to purchase agricultural machinery and other equipment needed by the settlers. After completing their payments, the settlers will receive full title as private owners of the land. Thus they will have changed their status from landless peasants with a reserved right to land in an ejido to private landowners.

This method was first tried in the Chapacao region of northern Veracruz, where about 1,200 families have been settled on 74,000 acres of national lands since the beginning of 1959. The settlers received about 62 acres of cropland and an urban lot on which to build a house, have a vegetable garden, and keep a few chickens and other animals. The cost of building a typical two-room house is estimated at $96, using the labor of the settlers and machinery made available by the government.

In the case of new settlements under the ejido system, settlers repay to the government all the expenses mentioned above but do not pay for the land. On the other hand, they are given only limited possession of the land and not full title as under the Colonization Law.

- 5 -

According to the Agrarian Department, large tracts of national lands are available in the southeastern States of Tabasco, Campeche, and Chiapas. It is hoped that the settlers will come principally from the Central Plateau, thus relieving the pressure of population in that region.

New Interior Regulations for the Department of Agrarian and Colonization Affairs were published in the Diario Oficial for July 1, 1960. According to these new regulations the Department is in charge not only of the distribution of land under the ejido and colonization programs, but also of planning and promoting agricultural and livestock production in the ejidos and colonies, with the technical cooperation of the Ministry of Agriculture and Animal Industry. The Department is also charged with promoting the development of such industrial activities in the ejidos as may be complementary to agricultural production. These functions have been entrusted to the General Bureau of Ejido Agricultural Promotion. The Bureau is one of 11 such bureaus established by the new regulations within the Department, the other 10 having the following functions: Administration; legal affairs; lands and waters; agrarian rights, agrarian organization in the ejidos; agricultural and livestock inaffectibility; inspection and claims; statistics, programs, and censuses; colonization; national and idle lands. The new regulations became effective 3 days after publication.

The Agrarian Department has announced that it is examining concessions of livestock inaffectibility to determine whether the concessionaires are fulfilling the conditions under which the concessions were made. These conditions include maintaining a certain number of head of livestock and delivering a certain portion of the calf crop to the ejidos in the neighborhood. Concessions of livestock inaffectibility are made for a period of 25 years and may be renewed for another similar period. During the period of the concession, the land included in the concession is not subject to expropriation under the agrarian laws. The Department has stated that when concessionaires are fulfilling the requirements of the law their concessions will be respected. At the same time the Department has announced that small private crop and livestock holdings within the limits established by the agrarian legislation and the Mexican Constitution will continue to be respected.

Land Distributed

The area distributed under the ejido program from its beginning in 1915 up to the present time amounts to about 98 million acres, granted to about 1,900,000 individuals. Relatively, this means that 27 percent of the total area of the country and 44 percent of all the cropland is now held by ejidatarios, who represent more than half of all the farmers in the country.

The program started very slowly while the nation's leaders debated the objectives to be achieved and the best methods of implementing them. With the beginning of the administration of President Lázaro Cárdenas in 1934, however, the program gathered considerable momentum. The amount of land distributed during his term of office represents more than 40 percent of the total area granted in the 45 years since the initiation of the program in 1915.

Table 1.--Mexico: Classification of grants by types of land 1/

	1915-1955	1955-1956	1956-1957	1957-1958	1958-1959	Total 1915-1959
	1,000 ha.	1,000 ha.	1,000 ha.	1,000 ha.	1,000 ha.	1,000 ha.
Cropland						
Irrigated or humid..........	1,492.3	8.8	10.7	5.2	2.9	1,519.9
Dry............	7,986.7	121.2	118.3	95.7	95.9	8,417.8
Total..........	9,479.0	130.0	219.0	100.9	98.8	9,937.7
Pastures.........	17,824.5	282.4	207.4	224.2	209.4	18,747.9
Woodland.........	8,870.6	117.2	146.9	208.3	198.6	9,541.6
Other...........	540.5	1.3	2.4	1.0	1.4	546.6
Total..........	36,714.6	530.9	485.7	534.4	508.2	38,773.8

1/ Includes only grants by restitution, dotación, and amplification.
1 hectare = 2.471 acres.

Source: Departamento Agrario.

After the end of the Cárdenas administration, however, the area distributed each year declined, but the administration of President López Mateos,
which took office on December 1, 1958, has greatly intensified it. During
his first year in office, more than 2 million acres were granted.

Lands held by ejidos are fairly well distributed throughout the country,
but the greatest concentration is in the Central Plateau. Approximately 45
percent of the area in farms in the central region is held by ejidos. The
highest concentration is in the State of Morelos, just south of Mexico City,
where the 1950 Census shows that 83 percent of the total area of the State
is held by ejidos. The lowest concentration is in the arid, north-central
area, where livestock production is the principal use of the land. In
Coahuila and Sonora, for example, only 14 percent of the land is in ejidos.
Part of this land is not tillable and is not suitable, therefore, for distribution to ejidos in small plots.

During 1958-59, lands granted to new centers of population rose to
310,000 hectares (767,000 acres), almost nine times the level of the previous year; and lands delivered to settlers under the Colonization Law
reached almost 250,000 hectares (618,000 acres), more than 2-1/2 times the
previous year. In fact, lands distributed by these two new methods more
than equalled the grants by restitution, dotación, and amplification that
year.

Table 2.--Mexico: Distribution of land under the agrarian program,
1957-58 and 1958-59

Type	1957-58	1958-59
Grants by restitution, dotación, and amplification.....................	Hectares 534,401	Hectares 508,167
Communal lands.........................	182,460	80,177
New centers of population (crops)......	38,867	53,837
New centers of population (livestock only).................................		256,507
Total granted to ejidos..............	755,728	898,688
National lands........................	133,353	30,842
Lands delivered to settlers under the Colonization Law.....................	92,000	249,568
Total area distributed 1/............	981,081	1,179,098

1/ A large proportion of these totals consisted of pastures and woodland.
1 hectare = 2.471 acres.

Of the total granted to new centers of population in 1958-59, however,
only 53,837 hectares (133,000 acres) were cropland. The remaining 256,507
hectares (634,000 acres) represented the Cananea Ranch in northern Sonora,
which was expropriated in the previous administration and distributed by the
new administration. The grant was made to 853 families organized into seven
ejidos, considered as seven "new centers of population". The lands were
mostly pasture lands and the ejidos established were the first livestock
ejidos under the agrarian program. About half of the members of the ejidos
were already in the area and the remainder were brought principally from
other parts of the State of Sonora as well as from the Laguna region and
other northern districts.

Land Systems That Led to Reform

All of these reform measures were made necessary by the systems of land
tenure and holdings that developed over the years, many of which were so en-
trenched that the small farmer had no opportunity to obtain any land of his
own. At the time of the Spanish Conquest, for example, a form of land
tenure was already growing in importance whereby land was granted to the
head of a clan, to warriors, and to priests. In order to free these persons
for their specific duties, the land was tilled for them by other members of
the clan. These grants gradually became larger and they were tilled by
serfs called "mayeques".

- 8 -

The Spaniards, on gaining control of the country, took measures not only to protect the land-holding villages already existing in the country, but also to establish new ones. These new land-holding villages were patterned after the towns of Castile with which the conquerors were familiar. The Spanish legislation for Mexico, or New Spain as the country was then called, provided that the Indian towns should have an ejido, including cropland, woods, and pastures. These lands were to be administered by the town council. The ejido resembled in many ways the Indian altepetlalli.

The Spanish Crown established other forms of land tenure which were later to encroach upon the land-holding villages. The most important of these was the encomienda. It consisted of assigning in trust one or more villages to an individual with the right to collect tribute from the inhabitants and to require certain personal services from them. The encomiendas were usually granted to the conquistadores as a reward for their exploits and carried the obligation on the part of the recipient to Christianize the Indians under his jurisdiction and to protect them. Gradually this system developed into a feudalistic type of land tenure and the Indians became serfs on the property.

Some of these holdings were of tremendous size including many towns; however, many included only one village and its adjoining land. When requests for encomiendas became more numerous, there were cases of a village being divided between two or more. They were the origin of many Mexican haciendas or large estates. Another source was the estates held by Indian chieftains defeated by the Spaniards who replaced the former as masters of the land and the serfs attached to it. These large holdings tended to remain intact through the custom of creating mayorazgos, or entailed estates. A Spanish settler on acquiring a fortune usually requested a title of nobility from the Spanish Crown. The title was assigned to the estate, which then had to remain undivided. This custom prevailed throughout the colonial period and was largely responsible for the preservation of large estates in Mexico.

Independence from Spain in 1821 brought little change in the land holding pattern. In subsequent years, some increase took place in the number of landowners as a result of the abolition of the mayorazgos, and through the nationalization of church property and its sale to individuals.

From 1876 to 1910, however, this trend was reversed. The great prosperity in the country increased the demand for land. Therefore the government enacted a law in 1883 which authorized surveying companies to locate and measure idle lands, for which the companies were compensated with one-third of the lands surveyed. They were also given the privilege of purchasing the other two-thirds at special rates. This law resulted in the accumulation of vast holdings of land by the surveying companies. Most of this land was held in large tracts for speculative purposes. This land grabbing process was greatly accelerated in 1894 when a so-called Law of Colonization was adopted. It provided that any person could acquire idle or unclaimed lands without any limit as to the amounts and without any requirement that the lands be settled. The law also provided for grants of land to be made to individuals or companies, supposedly for the purpose of colonization. It has been estimated that during this period public lands representing 27 percent of the total area of the country were transferred to private hands in large blocks. These developments greatly strengthened the hacienda system and multiplied the discontent of the farmers, thus paving the way for revolt.

Effect of the Agrarian Reform Program

Following the Revolution in the early days of the reform movement, there was much confusion and a reduction in agricultural output as the new system got under way. Over the years, however, the reform program has been an important factor in the economic development of the country. The program ended the land monopoly and broke the power of the landed aristocracy that ruled Mexico before the Revolution; it also freed the farm workers from the economic bonds that attached them to the haciendas, and gave them the mobility which brought so many of them to the cities in search of industrial employment. Great progress has been made in improving agricultural techniques, increasing yields, and diversifying agricultural production. The rise in agricultural output has been particularly significant during the past 2 decades. The volume produced at the present time is three times that of 20 years ago, while population has increased by 76 percent in the same period.

However, the ejidos are not as productive as private farms; yields per acre on the ejidos are in most cases 20 to 25 percent lower. Among the chief reasons for these lower yields are: The small area of the plots, which in many cases results in an uneconomic use of the land; the lower educational level of the ejido population, with the consequent slower acceptance of improved methods; and the smaller capital resources available per unit of area, which also accounts in large measure for the lower level of techniques.

Although almost half of the irrigated area of Mexico is held by ejidos, the proportion of the cultivated area that is lost, principally because of drought, is 18 percent for the ejidos and only 8 percent for private holdings. Much of the area being farmed by the ejidos lacks sufficient rainfall for crop production and would be more suited for pastures or forests. Only 4 percent of the cultivated land on ejidos receives fertilizer, while this percentage is 7 for private holdings. The proportion of agricultural machinery in the ejidos also is much smaller than in private holdings. Of the total value of all machinery and equipment (including plows, tractors, cultivators, balers, trucks, etc.) in 1950 only 28 percent was in the ejidos and the remaining 72 percent in private holdings.

However, because of the large proportion of the cropland which it holds, the ejido is an important source of many of the leading crops produced in Mexico. Ejido farms produce more than 70 percent of the tobacco, more than 60 percent of the wheat, rice, sesame, and henequen, and more than 40 percent of the corn, beans, sugarcane, barley, and bananas. Therefore, the future development of Mexican agriculture depends to a great extent on the situation in the ejidos. Raising crop yields on lands held by the ejidos is one of the most important problems facing Mexico today, since on its solution depends not only the supply of many important commodities, but the welfare of a large segment of the rural population of the country.

The redistribution of the rural population is a promising development, as is also the technical and financial help that is being made available along with the land. Experience in the operation and implementation of the agrarian reform program is showing up some of its weaknesses and is paving the way for a sounder program for the future.

Growth Through Agricultural Progress